D0555824

Silke Vry

Paul Klee
for Children

PRESTEL

Munich · London · New York

Goldfish, 1925, Hamburger Kunsthalle

For Stefan

"Create goals for yourself:
play, fool yourself and others, be an artist."

(Paul Klee, Diary, 1902)

Contents

Klee – Lucky Clover

Come along, let's visit the painter with the lovely last name of Klee, which is German for "clover." His full name is Paul Klee.

Clover and good **luck belong** together. Whoever finds a lucky clover, a four-leaf clover, is lucky because the wish that person makes will come true.

Paul Klee felt his wishes had come true when he painted. And he created his pictures with the aim of making us happy, inspiring us to **dream** and carrying us off into another, more beautiful world...

Isn't that a lovely aim?! How nice of Mr. "Lucky Clover" to think of your happiness, and mine, too.

If Klee saw you in front of one of his paintings right now, he'd definitely be happy. He'd be envious of you for being a child. And perhaps he would ask you for your advice on how to paint or draw a picture. Yes, he really might! That's because he truly believed that children are great artists. All children, including you! So even if you think you aren't any good at drawing or painting, don't despair. Often Paul thought he wasn't much good at it himself. So if you're curious to learn more about Klee, the journey can begin.

Have you got everything you need? Pen? Paper? Then let's have some fun. Be prepared to create your own pictures. You and Mr. Klee may even make art together!

Motif from Hammamet, 1914,
Kunstmuseum Basel

It's Me, Päuli!

left: Paul Klee, Bern 1880,
Zentrum Paul Klee, Bern,
Gift of the Klee family

Even a great artist was once a little kid. As little as you, as me, as all of us once were:

The picture above shows Paul Klee just after his first birthday.
Sweet, isn't he?

"First, I was a child. Then I wrote nice essays and could do sums, too," he later wrote in his diary. If you look at the photograph above, you can see that even when he was a child, Paul faced the world with a serious expression on his face. And if you compare this photograph with the one on page 30, you can see that Paul was just as serious years later, when he was a grown-up. Paul looked out at the world with his big, beautiful brown eyes. He already had those eyes as a child, of course.

Klee's mother and sister called him "Päuli," which means "little Paul" in Swiss German. The Klee family was made up of Paul, his sister Mathilde (who was three years older than he was), his mother Ida, and his father Hans. They all lived in a pretty city called Bern, which is in Switzerland.

The Klee family had moved to Bern when Paul was a couple of months old. He had been born in a small town called München-buchsee, which is near Bern, on December 18th, 1879.

Paul and Mathilde Klee, ca. 1884,
Zentrum Paul Klee, Bern,
Gift of the Klee family

But Paul was not entirely Swiss. His mother was from Switzerland, but his father was from Germany. So Paul was partly German. That was a shame, because being German almost cost him his life when he was a young man. (You can read more about this part of Paul's history on page 65).

Paul Klee, 1892, Zentrum Paul Klee, Bern, Gift of the Klee family

Being such a young person is a strange thing. Paul had the impression that the world in which he lived belonged entirely to adults. He felt that it was **the grown-ups who were important, and the children who were unimportant.** So unimportant, in fact, that they were only taken seriously when they became as much like grown-ups as possible. But hopefully that would never happen to him!

Paul often felt that nobody understood him, and that he was not being taken seriously. When he got dressed up, drew a picture, or hummed a little tune to himself, he was sometimes teased. And when he was teased, it was always by an adult, of course!

Over the next few years, Paul slowly grew up – there wasn't anything he could do to stop it! On the outside, at least, he looked more and more like an adult. But he also decided to take refuge as often as he could in his inner, better world. Here, he was a child and would stay a child for his whole life.

How did he get to this inner world? It's quite simple: **all he had to do was close his eyes!**

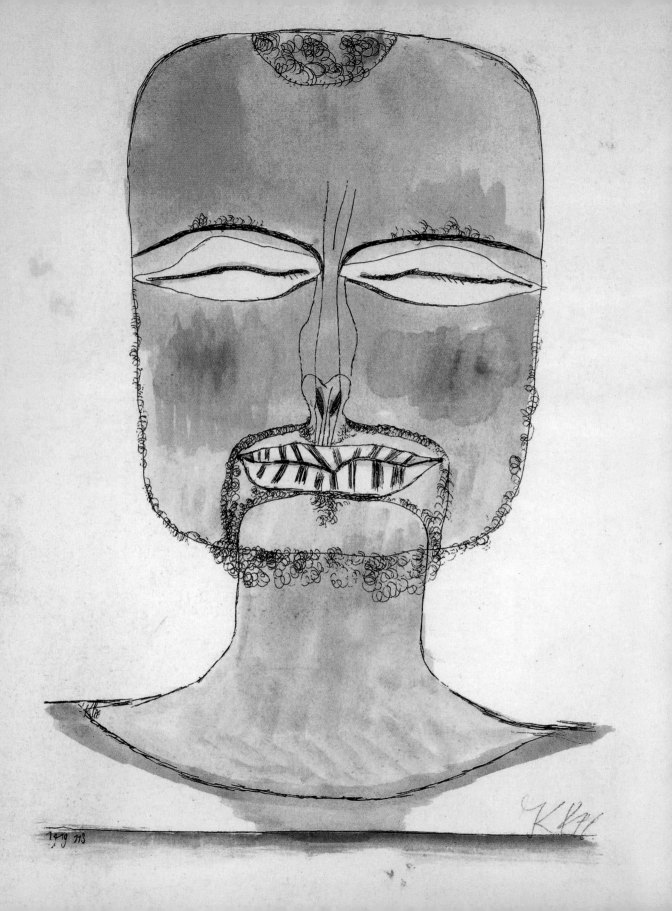

The World Within

Try closing your eyes for a moment ... But not right now! First read what it says here.

When you close your eyes, try to imagine something in particular. You can start with something easy, such as your last birthday cake. What? You didn't have a birthday cake? Then you can have one now: just imagine one ...
That was easy, wasn't it?

Then you might imagine you are exploring your home. Walk through the rooms, open one door and then another, uncover secret drawers. Now open the front door, walk outside, and keep following your nose. Sooner or later on this imaginary journey, you'll reach places you have never come across before.

What now?

This time, **don't imagine what is really there,** but imagine what **could be** there. Are there houses with colorful decorations, wondrous trees, or green-and-red-checkered birds? Anything is possible! And some of it is better than the unpleasant things of real life, such as **accidents or bad grades at school!**

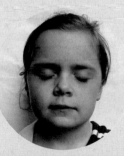

left:
Absorption, 1919, Albertina, Vienna

A self-portrait with closed eyes: Paul Klee was convinced that the world inside of us is much more wonderful than the world we can see using our eyes. Klee wanted to explore this wonderful world and record it in his pictures.

Ask somebody to take a photograph of you with your eyes closed while you are on one of your imaginary journeys. The photo probably wouldn't look like any other one you have! If you like it, you could stick it in the space to the left. And perhaps you would like to show what your family and friends might look like while traveling in their minds?

Can You See What is Within?

Surprising things can be found within the mind. But you can also make important discoveries by looking inside the "bodies" of objects.

Imagine that you can see through the outer layer of any object you choose. Just think of all the things you would find there. Completely unknown worlds would open up to you, and entirely familiar objects would suddenly appear strange and unusual. You might find yourself on a miniature "space flight."

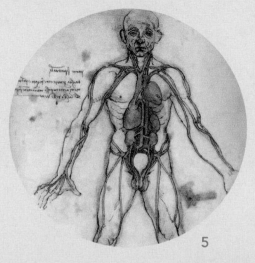

5

2

1

Can you work out which objects we are looking inside of?

Can you match the pictures with the correct words?

But watch out:

there are more words than pictures,

so you will have to make sure you choose the right ones.

If you then arrange the matched words and pictures from 1 to 6,

you will find that the letters after the words

will spell out a special word.

Turn to page 85 to see if you have figured out the correct word.

Read about it on page 85

Computer · **M**
Car · **T**
Clockwork · **I**
Canalization · **H**
Red cabbage · **A**
Battery · **C**
Human · **E**
Tree · **L**
Earth · **G**
Onion · **S**

The special word is: _ _ _ _ _ _ _

3

4

6

By looking at familiar objects in unusual and new ways, we can make those objects seem more exciting. You can even make a game out this activity at your next birthday party. Turn to page 85 to discover how.

What isn't on the "inside" is on the "outside" ... Understanding Klee

Just imagine what you would get to see if you could look not just beneath the surface of an object, but deep within another person! What if you could see not only that person's muscles and blood vessels, but also things that no one else could: thoughts, fantasies, and dreams ...

That sounds complicated, doesn't it? And it isn't exactly easy, either ... Doctors, for example, can see through us and have a good look at our insides using an X-ray machine. The resulting picture shows our bones and organs, but you won't find our thoughts there, no matter how hard you look.

Intention, 1938,
Museum of Fine Arts Bern

Painters can do what machines are not capable of: they can make thoughts — and lots of other invisible things — visible.

That is just what Paul Klee did in the painting on page 12. But what is he showing here? A **jumble of symbols?** You probably can't make out much in it, other than the strange shapes and symbols. Is this picture anything more than a mysterious jumble? **Actually, if you look closely, you can read and understand the painting.**

In the middle, towards the left, is half a human figure. Can you spot the person's head, eye, mouth, hair, shoulder, chest, and arm?

To the left and right of the figure are many strange symbols. The left side is darker than the right because this is where we can see those things that people leave behind. **Every symbol represents a thought or a memory of friends and encounters.** We can make out a tree, a dog, flags, and lots of other things. Can you see how crowded it all is? Just like our memories.

No matter how clear the thoughts and plans are, they look as though they have not been thought all the way through to completion: one cannot really make things out properly. You can change that. Complete the mysterious symbols to make meaningful objects. You can do that on page 85.

You may also notice that things are a bit less crowded within the figure. Here, too, there are strange symbols, but they are better organized. There is more space and they keep their distance from each other. This is the "inside" of a person. The person's thoughts, plans, and intentions are shown here. Paul Klee probably captured himself in this painting. In other words, the figure represents him. He uses the painting to let us see into his inner world.

Klee and Clover

Most people know what clover is. They may not know that Paul Klee's surname is the German word for "clover," of course. But most everybody has seen green clover, which grows just about everywhere in the summer.

Trifolium Pratense, clover: Because it normally has three leaves, the clover's scientific name begins with *Trifolium*. Only the unusual four-leaf type is lucky, though.

Clover is easy to recognize and easy to like. It looks attractive, and it even carries the promise of good fortune.

Paul Klee loved nature in all of its manifestations. He thought that anybody who wants to be an artist must also be a naturalist, just like him. Because Klee wanted to have the greatest possible understanding of nature and the laws that govern it, he observed and studied it very carefully. And part of this work, of course, included studying the plant that shared his name. Sometimes, Paul drew a clover on his pictures as a way of signing his name.

Herbarium Leaves, 1930, Zentrum Paul Klee, Bern, Gift of the Klee family

Read about it on page 86

You can "collect" nature by drying and pressing plants and sticking them into an album (called a "herbarium"). Turn to page 86 to find out exactly how.

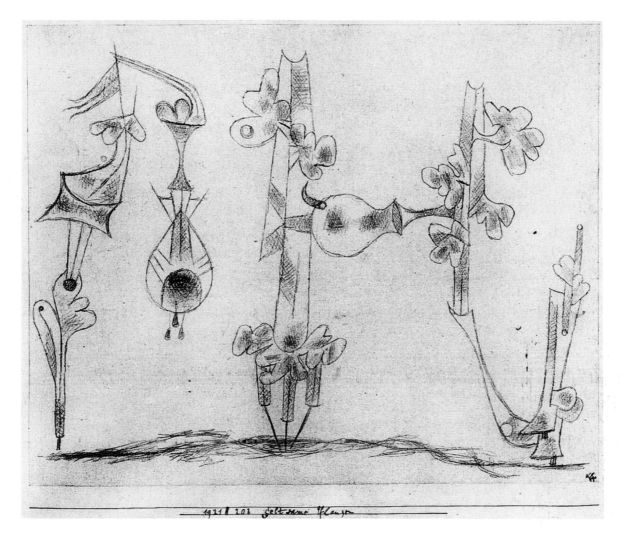

Strange Plants, 1921,
Kunstsammlung Nordrhein-Westfalen, Düsseldorf

Do you know all about clover?

1. How many different types of clover are there worldwide?

    a) 3   b) 12   c) 243 ?

2. What does it mean if you say that somebody "is in clover"?

Read about it on page 86

3. Sometimes, there are more than four leaves on a single plant.
The record number of leaves is currently

    a) 7   b) 18   c) 25

Grandmother's Coloring Pencils

Paul loved to visit his grandmother. Like most grandmothers, she only wanted the best for her grandson.

"When it came to toilet paper, she used particularly soft kinds on me, so-called silk paper," Klee would write in his diary later on. And she did something else for him, too: she showed him how to use coloring pencils. She herself loved to embroider and draw. As soon as Paul sat down with her, he reached for her coloring pencils and paper and started to draw.

What happened then was mysterious and strange. It could hardly be put into words: suddenly, the piece of paper in front of him was no longer white. It was covered with something he had created, something that had not yet been there moments before. He could look at it again and again, hang it on his grandmother's kitchen wall, and even take it home. In these moments, he felt happy and powerful. And he had an inkling of future happiness.

Childhood drawing of Paul Klee (*Presenting a Bouquet to Mme. Grenouillet*), 1883/1884, private collection, Switzerland, stored at the Zentrum Paul Klee, Bern

Childhood artwork of Paul Klee (*Four Flowers*), private collection, Switzerland, stored at the Zentrum Paul Klee, Bern

right: Childhood artwork of Paul Klee (*Church, the Clock with Invented Numerals*), 1883/1884, Zentrum Paul Klee, Bern

In this way, Klee could create the whole world anew ...

That was a completely new feeling for him. For nobody in Paul's home drew or painted. Some of them played music, which was lovely. But as soon as a note had been played or sung, it disappeared again. It isn't possible to capture the sounds of music the way you can capture the lines and colors of a picture.

What Paul particularly liked about his grandmother was that she didn't criticize his drawings. Quite the opposite! She always encouraged him to keep drawing. Even when Klee was completely dissatisfied with one of his pictures, possibly because it didn't look at all like the thing he was trying to draw, his grandmother would find something positive in it.

When did you last draw something? It's true that drawing is not always an entirely pleasant experience, especially when you're not at all satisfied with the result, like Paul. But don't despair. Instead, try this: after you complete a drawing, write your name and the date on the finished picture. Then later on, have another person look at your work of art. Just don't throw it away! Paul hardly ever threw any of his drawings away ...

Chocolate Pudding Art

Do you really, really like chocolate pudding? If so, you are like most people. Obviously, those who love chocolate pudding feel there is never enough of it, and they clean every last scrap off their plates. The result usually looks something like this:

Paul Klee, too, sometimes ate chocolate pudding. One day, when he was scraping the white porcelain plate with his spoon, he left white marks against the dark background. He must have thought: what wonderful effects can be achieved in this way! How unusual and exciting! And soon, his empty pudding plate must have looked something like this:

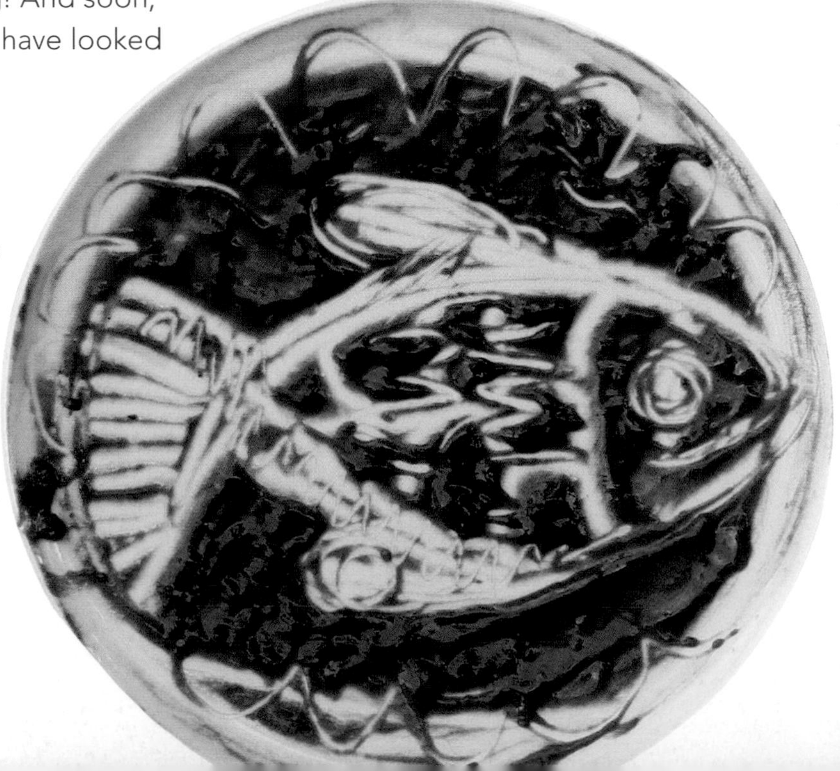

But you can't live on chocolate pudding, and pictures made of leftover dessert don't keep forever. And so another technique had to be found in which white lines could play the main part in a picture, shining out against a dark surface.

My Father, 1906, Zentrum Paul Klee, Bern, Gift of Livia Klee

When Paul was an adult, he developed such a technique with glass -- the reverse-glass scratch painting technique. On May 10th, 1905, Klee wrote a long letter full of enthusiasm to his friend Lily, telling her about his discovery:

"This is how I did it: I covered a pane of glass in black (using India ink), placed it on a sheet of white paper, and then scratched away the ink with a needle, so that the white paper began to shine through. In this way, I exposed the light and the dark remained ..."

Read about it on page 86

What do you need to make a sweet chocolate picture like that? Chocolate pudding, of course! You can find instructions for making it on every box of chocolate pudding mix, or you can turn to page 86.

On page 86, you can also find out what you need to make a reverse-glass scratch painting.

Imaginary Journeys to Happiness

Paul with his uncle, the fattest man in Switzerland, 1886, Zentrum Paul Klee, Bern, Gift of the Klee family

When Paul Klee was nine years old, he wrote in his diary:

"In the restaurant belonging to my uncle, the fattest man in Switzerland, there were tables with polished marble slabs on whose surface you could see a jumble of petrified marbling. In this labyrinth of lines, you could make out grotesque human forms, and copy them using a pencil. I was obsessed with this ..."

Yes, you need to stimulate your imagination. And if you are lucky, the simplest, most everyday things can lead you into the most beautiful, fantastical worlds and inspire you to create the most unbelievable drawings. You can find shapes in everyday objects that you would otherwise not have come up with on your own ...

Paul Klee had a special talent for seeing the unusual in the ordinary world. When he was young, Paul often found many exciting shapes in his uncle's restaurant ... all while holding an ice cream in one hand and a pencil in the other!

And now it is your turn!

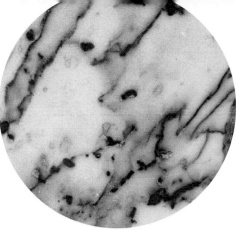

What can you see in the jumble of lines to the right?
A face, a landscape, a monster?
Anything is possible if your imagination allows it.
(If you don't happen to be sitting
in front of a marble tabletop,
a glance at a cloud-filled sky will do the trick.)
Find out more on page 87.

Read about it on page 87

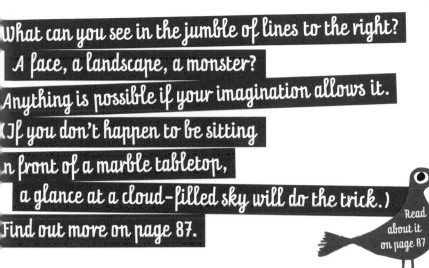

By the way, other great artists used similar "tricks" to prompt their painterly imagination, too. Some threw a wet sponge at the workshop wall or made blotches of paint here, there, and everywhere when they ran out of ideas. These blotches sometimes gave rise to shapes and figures that could never have been invented in any other way.

Satirical drawing in an exercise book (German literature) belonging to Paul Klee, 1897, private collection, Switzerland, stored at the Zentrum Paul Klee, Bern

21

What a Naughty Boy!

Sitting at the table, behaving nicely, drawing pictures: Is that what a great artist's childhood looks like?

Well, Paul could make art in this way when he was at peace with himself and with the world around him. And then the grown-ups would praise him: "Well done, Paul!" But the grown-ups always expected him to be well-mannered, and there were times when Paul felt they were too strict with him. There were also times when Paul felt himself superior to other people. In these moments, the outside world came into conflict with Paul's inner world, and he could **behave differently. Very differently!**

At such moments, he would rebel and express the other sides of his personality ... the dark parts of Paul that needed to get out.

Girl with Doll, 1905,
Zentrum Paul Klee, Bern

Read for yourself:

"I would sometimes deliberately cause minor injuries to a little girl who was not pretty and wore an apparatus because of her crooked legs. Thinking the whole family, and the mother in particular, inferior, I would pretend to be a good boy and ask those responsible to entrust the sweet little thing to me for a short walk. We would walk a short distance peacefully, holding hands. Soon, when we reached the nearby field on which the potatoes blossomed and the little ladybirds were to be found, or sometimes even before we got there, we would walk one behind the other. At the right moment, I would give my charge a gentle push. The poor thing fell over, and I would lead her back to her mother as she wailed. With an innocent expression, I would report that "She fell over." I repeated this maneuver several times without Mrs. Enger discovering the truth. I must have assessed her accurately."

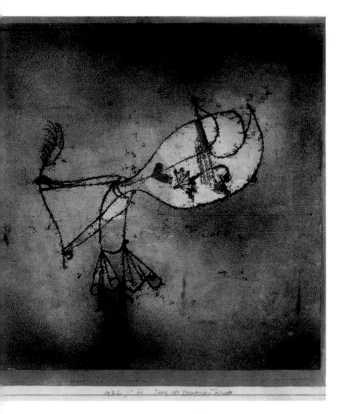

Dance of the Mourning Child, 1922,
Collection of Michael and Judy Steinhardt, New York

Klee wrote these lines down many years after the events took place. Obviously, he couldn't forget them.

Do you think he should have been ashamed of himself?

Has something like this ever happened to you? Has somebody treated you the way that Paul treated the little girl in this story ... cruelly and unfairly? Is there anybody you would like to write an angry letter to because they hurt your feelings?

Fugue in Red, 1921,
private collection, Switzerland

Violins?

Paul was still a little boy when his grand-mother died. The colorful afternoons at her house with paper and pencils were now over. Suddenly, nobody took care of his artistic education anymore. He could no longer entertain himself by drawing, and artistically he felt "completely orpha-ned," entirely abandoned. That is how he described it later in life.

But now, he started to get into some-thing that was new to him: **music.** Although he had often listened to his parents making music together, he had not yet managed to make proper music on an instrument himself.

What a pleasure it was when he found himself standing in front of his teacher with his own little violin. It didn't matter that the sounds he made on the strings did not please people straight away.

But that changed soon. By the time he was eleven years old, Paul played the violin so brilliantly that an orchestra from Bern allowed him to perform with them at concerts. Paul soon came to love music more than anything else. He often felt that it touched his soul in a way that nothing else could, not even his drawings and paintings.

Why was this the case?

It is quite simple, really: drawings and paintings usually show something specific, such as a person, a landscape, or some object or other. If you want to see these things, you have to look at the picture – you have to **open your eyes!**

To listen to music, you need nothing but your ears, and you can just close your eyes! Once you have done that, you become more at one with yourself and you enter your inner world. Music reaches you in this way and there is nothing you can do to stop it. After all, you can't simply close your ears in the way that you can close your eyes. Paul noticed something else about music, too. When a person hears music that is written to describe something – such as a gushing river or a lost coin – a picture of that scene or object is created inside the person. It doesn't exist anywhere else.

Once the music dies away, the picture disappears as well. Paul Klee was amazed when he realized this fact – that music can describe pictures without using the pictures themselves. In other words, music can describe pictures that don't actually exist.

That is why music can touch the soul.

And that is exactly what Paul decided to achieve with his pictures. He decided to use colors and shapes in his paintings to create something like the distinctive sounds of a piece of music, which relies on notes, keys, rhythms, and lots of other things. If only he could make his pictures sing …

Making music yourself is such fun. Why not make a simple musical instrument yourself? You can read how to do it on page 87.

Have another look at Klee's self-portrait on page 8. As you already know, he has closed his eyes in order to absorb himself completely in his inner world. To make it even clearer that he does not want to be disturbed, Paul has simply left out two things. Have you noticed what those things are? The answer is on page 87.

Read about it on page 87

... or Poetry?

Anybody who wants to be a painter must also be a naturalist, philosopher, and even a poet. Paul Klee was completely convinced of this.

Writing poetry means: choosing and combining words, and not too many, in such a way that they create a little story or allegory. The words are chosen in such a way that you don't just hear them, you also see something in your mind's eye. In other words, writing poetry means "painting" with words.

When Paul Klee needed a word that did not exist yet, he simply invented one. He named some of his pictures using words that he had thought up himself. Klee chose these words so that you could immediately "see" a particular picture upon hearing them:

**twittering machine, chair animal, windmill blossoms ...
and he named a far-away land that he longed for (although he had never been there) BERIDE.**

If you have as many talents as Paul Klee did, sooner or later you have to answer the difficult question: what on earth should I be when I grow up? How shall I earn money when I'm older? No matter how much he loved painting with words, would he be able to support a family in this way? How many words would he need in order to raise a little Felix?

Read about it on page 88

Now it's your turn:
What do you think Paul Klee might have invented the word "Lomolarm" to describe?

Does it describe ...
a) ... a small yellow bird?
b) ... a slow-moving railway engine?
c) ... a sad face?

Landscape with Yellow Birds, 1923,
private collection, Switzerland

The birds are to be envied,
They avoid
Thinking about the tree and the roots
Agile, self-contended, all day long they swing.

Paul Klee

Read
about it
on page 88

Try to write a short poem yourself. Don't worry, you can do it. Maybe some instructions will be helpful? You can find those on page 88, as well as a space in which to write your poem.

My Place, 1896,
Zentrum Paul Klee, Bern

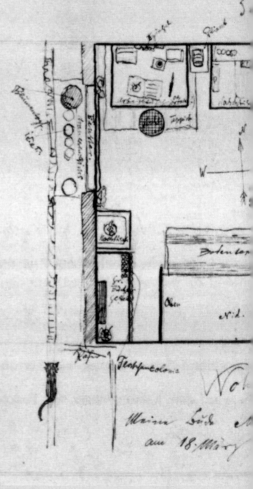

At Home
with Paul Klee,
Welcome,
Come In!

Paul Klee had his own room, and in this drawing he proudly shows us what it looked like. You can see that it is made with love. And it has everything you might need: a bed, a table, a chair, a shelf. What more could anyone want?

Paul, at least, needed nothing more. He sat at the table to do his homework, to write poems and stories, and to draw. Can you make out the bookshelf behind the bed? It's practical: he hung pieces of fabric in front of it so that he could quickly make the place look tidy for unexpected visitors. All he had to do was draw the curtain.

This room is where Klee kept all of his treasures, including his books and his collection of insects. If you want to know what else was to be found in Paul's room, you can have a look at the floor plan that he drew. It shows what the furniture would have looked like if he had seen it from above.

Have you ever tried to make a picture like this of your room, a so-called floor plan? Have a go. Turn to page 88 to find out how.

Read about it on page 88

Floor Plan, 1897,
Zentrum Paul Klee, Bern

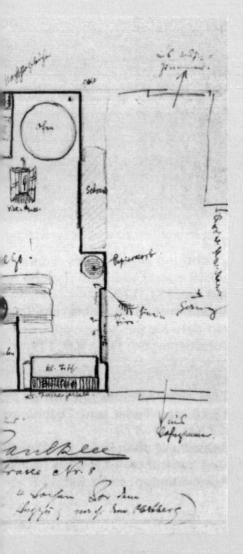

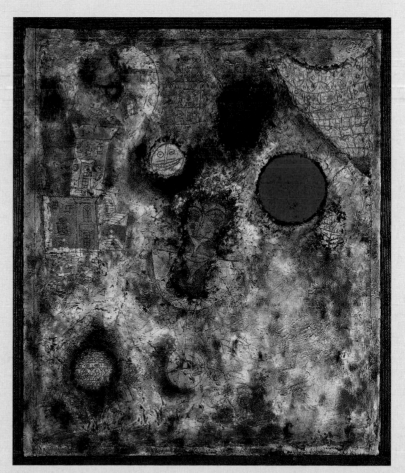

Magic Garden, 1926, The Solomon R. Guggenheim Foundation, Peggy Guggenheim Collection, Venice

Paul Klee on a Postcard from the Gallery *Der Sturm*, 1916

Painting and Becoming Human in Munich

Paul was certain of just one thing: he had to leave Bern, leave Switzerland, and go somewhere that was **"bigger, more interesting, and more lively."** He decided to go to Munich. At the time, Munich was the most important city in Germany for artists. But as much as Paul cared about art, what really appealed to him about Munich was the thought of getting as far away as possible very soon.

Klee only wanted to do those things that really meant something to him. He called this plan **"becoming human."** Paul felt that the most important thing for an artist was to master the art of living.

So what did Paul Klee decide to do to achieve fame and fortune?

At first, he didn't believe he could use any of his talents to become famous, or even earn enough money to make a living.

"Fame as a painter? Author? Modern poet?? Bad joke."

Have you ever wanted to be somewhere quite different? Perhaps you would like to live in a particular place because the sun looks especially beautiful there when it sets above the ocean? Maybe you would be allowed to eat ice cream all day long if you were there? You can draw the place of your dreams — or stick a photograph of it — here.

But what did "becoming human" mean for Paul Klee? It meant something like this: letting himself, his feelings, and his thoughts grow like a delicate plant. Sometimes he might wait in agony for a "blossom" to appear, but he would always remain full of hope that his life would be guided in the right direction. In addition to "becoming human," Paul remained his parents' obedient son. Once he had arrived in Munich, he obediently took his drawings to the Academy of Fine Arts. After all, his Papa had given him money so that he could study. And then, at last, he reached his goal: **Franz von Stuck** became his teacher. He was the painter that everyone said you had to learn from if you wanted to be successful. Franz von Stuck painted paintings that looked like this:

Paul, on the other hand, wanted to make pictures that looked something like this:

Franz von Stuck,
Sunset by the Sea, 1900,
Galerie Ritthaler, Munich

Paul Klee,
Sunken Landscape, 1918,
Museum Fokwang, Essen

31

Stuck did not understand Paul, and Paul did not understand Stuck, and it soon became clear that the arrangement would not work. How could the older artist teach his pupil about his art? And how on earth was Paul supposed to learn anything about color from this painter?

Full of disappointment, Klee wrote to his parents: **"Once again, I have ... realized that I can't paint."**
(It makes you want to comfort him: "Yes, Paul, you can paint!")
From then onwards, Klee started to spend more time drawing again. And he made sculptures, three-dimensional works of art. They looked like this:

Could this sculpture be a special kind of art? Maybe it's not just a sculpture, but both a sculpture and a drawing at the same time?

Read about it on page 89

Turn to page 89 to find out how to make drawings three dimensional.

Head Formed from a Piece of Brick smoothed by the River Lech, 1919, 33, Zentrum Paul Klee, Bern

32

One of Paul's wishes certainly did come true in Munich. He could tell at first glance that this city was livelier than any other place he had known. How different it was from Bern! Everybody and everything appeared to be in motion:

On the street, **automobiles** rushed by.

The first **cinemas** showed pictures that had been set in motion. These were some of the first movies, and the audiences hurried to get to the evening shows on time.

A World of Movement

And **waves** that moved through the air invisibly made "telegraphy" possible. This magical process involved transmitting words rapidly (and invisibly) between two places that were far apart.

No wonder people moved more quickly here than they did in Bern. **What a bustling, crazy time!**

It makes sense that artists, too, were impressed. Lots of them had recently begun to make movement the subject of their art.

Some painters showed almost nothing else in their pictures but brief snatches of time, **fleeting moments** such as laundry fluttering in the wind, dancers on a stage, and pedestrians hurrying by in the rain. Painters suddenly found these moments precious and worth painting – precisely because everything in life was changing so quickly.

Pablo Picasso, *Maya with Doll,* 1938, Musée Picasso, Paris

Gustave Chaillebotte, *Paris Street; Rainy Day,* 1877, Art Institute of Chicago

Other painters, who called themselves **Cubists,** made really strange paintings. These pictures made you think you were looking at the same things from different angles at the same time. A face could be shown from the left, from the front, and from the right, almost as though one had sped past it and seen it from several sides all at once.

Other artists made use of knowledge gained from movies, as well as from painted pictures that showed entire **sequences of movement** on a single canvas.

Read about it on page 89

You, too, can create movement in otherwise static pictures. Turn to page 89 to find out how.

Giacomo Balla, *Dynamism of a Dog on a Leash,* 1912, Museum of Modern Art, New York

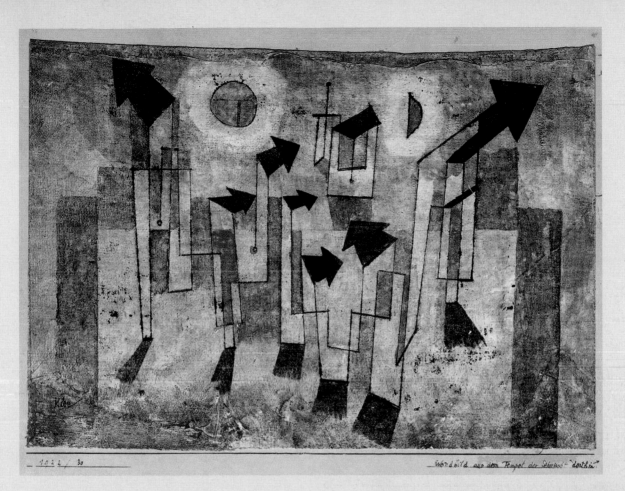

1922/ 30

Mural from the Temple of Longing Over There, 1922,
The Metropolitan Museum of Art, New York

Movement is Everything

Of course, Paul Klee was delighted by the art of many of his colleagues. But he didn't need to watch movies or look at cars driving by to feel that the entire world, and everything in it, was almost constantly in motion.

Paul could even feel motion in his mind. Yes, it's true! You can do the same by going on an imaginary journey. Imagine that you are taking a walk on the deck of a big ship that is sailing down a river. You are all by yourself, nobody else is around. Imagine the peace, the silence! Yes, it probably would be very quiet.

There are so many movements
that we hardly notice.
    Yet they take place nonetheless,
        and many of them are vital:
the beating of our heart,
the flowing of blood in our veins …
    Can you come up with anything else?
Think about it for a while,
    and then turn to page 90.

Read about it on page 90

And yet everything around you would be in motion: quiet, but full of energy. You would be able to feel some of this movement with your body, some of it you would be able to see, and some of it you would just sense because you would know it is taking place.

First, while you are walking, you are in motion. That's obvious! The wind blows in your face as you walk, while clouds drift past in the sky. And the ship is moving, too. (It might even be moving in the opposite direction to the one you are walking in. What a strange feeling!)

And don't forget the river, whose water flows in a particular direction. Even the Earth, on which all of this is taking place, keeps spinning around itself and making a yearly path around the sun – just as other planets travel around other stars across the universe.

In other words: everything is in motion!

Life means movement, after all! Only dead things don't move on their own.

All is White

When Paul Klee started to paint a new picture, and sat down in front of a white canvas or a gleaming piece of white paper, he often shook with fear: **it was so white!**

It was an enormous, unstructured nothing, absolutely frozen.

After all, you don't come across a really gleaming white object every day. Perhaps that is why pure white makes people feel unsettled. In fact, very few people paint their walls a pure white. Even smooth surfaces are usually given "rough fibers" to create structure, shadows, a visible "something."

If the surface of an image or object is white, it can both calm and distract a viewer.

To understand what is depicted in these white images, the eyes and the brain need to work things through and sort things out. Have a look for yourself.

Can you see the objects hidden here? The answers are on page 90.

Read about it on page 90

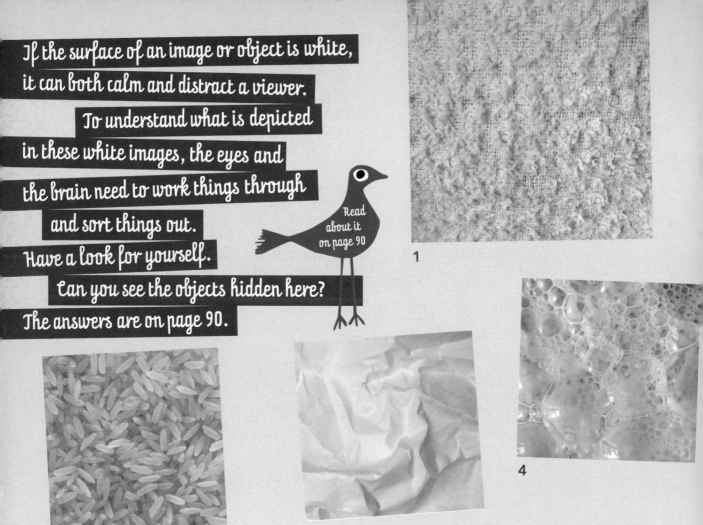

1

2

3

4

5

The smooth white did not just dazzle Paul's eyes, it also paralyzed his imagination. So what did he do about it?

Sometimes he painted colored shapes onto the reverse of the drawing paper. They could be seen through the paper and gave the front a touch of color. At other times, Klee crumpled up the paper before starting to draw. He would even apply a layer of "dirt" to the ground of his pictures.

Life and Love

... she loves him / she loves him not / she loves him!

"I love you as though you were my life blood ..."
Lily loves Paul, and Paul loves Lily!

Paul with Lily in the garden of his parents' house in Bern, 1906, Zentrum Paul Klee, Bern, Gift of the Klee family

First came the engagement, then the wedding. Paul and Lily made a beautiful couple. Yet soon they were no longer a twosome, but a little family – a three-leaf clover. Felix, whom they sometimes called Bubi (which means "little boy" in German), had arrived. And Paul, who had not long before written in his diary that **"I could do without having lots of children even more easily than I could do without good wine,"** had become a father himself.

Well, having just one additional mouth to feed hardly made his family one with "lots of **children**," but it certainly meant a lot of **work!** And as Lily continued to make money as a piano teacher – money they needed because Paul couldn't yet support a family from the sale of his paintings – Klee had to look after the baby by himself.

Paul was not just a loving father, but also a conscientious one. He made precise records of his son's progress in his "Felix Calendar": what the little boy ate and drank, how much weight he gained, how much weight he lost, whether he coughed or threw up, when he coughed or threw up, how high his temperature was, and everything else Paul experienced with his son.

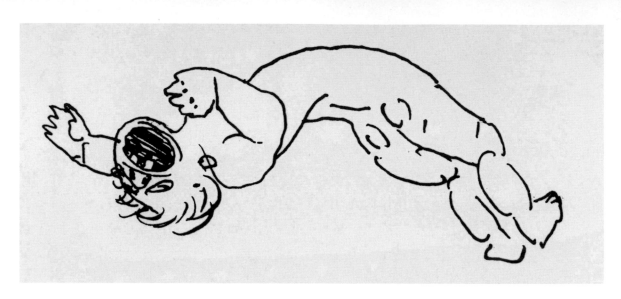

Crying Felix, 1908, Zentrum Paul Klee,
Bern, Gift of the Klee family

"Heating some water, adding a little milk, holding the bottle up to the eye, and then in through the open gate it goes! How greedily he drank! After that, he was quiet again."
"Bangs himself on the head repeatedly and laughs boisterously …"
"Says pa-pa and pa-pa-pa several times. Bad, very bad mood …"

"Severe temper tantrums cloud the picture slightly, for example when he is supposed to sit on his potty and doesn't want to. He then hits out at everything using both of his arms. But he is too young to be corrected. At the moment, he is sleeping sweetly in his little bed and you are fooled into thinking that one is looking at a little angel."

Paul Klee listened enthusiastically as his son "talked." His ears perked up, Paul sat in front of the little boy with a pen and a piece of paper and recorded every single gurgling noise with great interest and enthusiasm.

"Oli-yoli-yoli togedo, togedodo, todje-do!", "Ewrew-rew-ewrew"

Portrait of a Child (Felix), 1908,
Zentrum Paul Klee, Bern, Gift of Livia Klee

He wondered again and again: how were these curious noises created? And what did they mean? The phenomenon he was observing was wonderful, because one thing seemed clear: there appeared to be a source of energy deep inside this little creature. And the bizarre sounds bubbled up from that source constantly. Paul Klee was fascinated.

He felt that in this way, a child does something quite different from what grown-ups do when they speak. Grown-ups know a ready-made word for every possible object; and when grown-ups speak, they simply reproduce these words out of pure habit. For every object, they use a pre-assigned word.

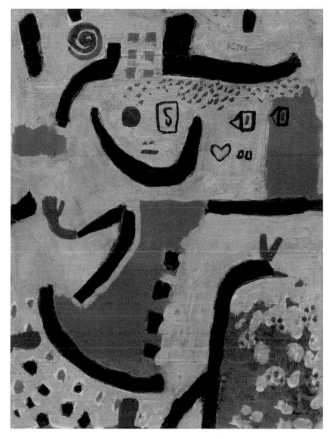

A Children's Game, 1939, National Gallery Berlin, Museum Berggruen

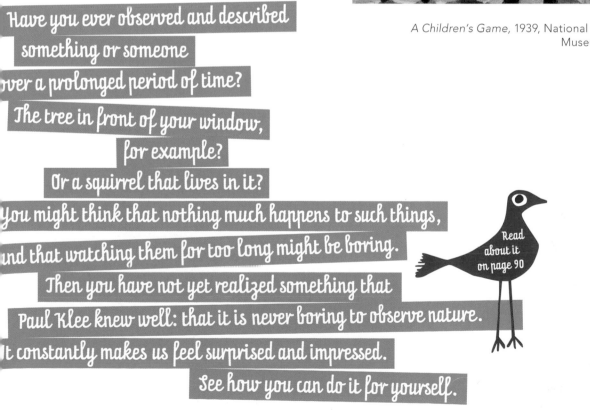

Have you ever observed and described something or someone over a prolonged period of time? The tree in front of your window, for example? Or a squirrel that lives in it? You might think that nothing much happens to such things, and that watching them for too long might be boring. Then you have not yet realized something that Paul Klee knew well: that it is never boring to observe nature. It constantly makes us feel surprised and impressed. See how you can do it for yourself.

Read about it on page 90

They call one thing a **"house,"** another a **"tree,"** and a third thing an **"apple."**

But when a newborn human begins to "babble" away, it simply babbles. It does not even expect to be understood by anybody. It just tries things out, feels pleased, changes things, tries again ... And that is what Paul was so fascinated by. He felt that art should be like that, too: artists should draw from their own innermost source, deep inside, and just go for it. They shouldn't care whether anybody understands them or not!

This is how German artist Caspar David Friedrich painted houses, trees, and clouds some 100 years before Klee:

In pictures, those innermost feelings could look something like this:

Intention (Details), 1938, Zentrum Paul Klee, Bern

Klee wondered whether you could observe a person's innermost source when watching a little child paint. A couple of years later, Paul gave Felix a paintbrush and paints, and indeed:

"The pictures painted by my little Felix are better than my own, which have often dripped through my brain…"

So one can learn a lot from children, as Paul Klee discovered once again.

There was nothing that Paul Klee wouldn't do for his baby Felix. In addition to cooking for him, taking his temperature, and keeping a diary, he did things that both of them enjoyed a great deal, such as playing with a puppet theater. For this, Paul designed and made hand puppets, each of which looked different from the rest. Father and son used the puppets to stage plays. In case you would like to try something similar, you can find out how it is done on page 90. Klee made one of his puppets to look like himself. Can you see which one that is?

Read about it on page 90

Group portrait hand puppets, 1916–1925, Zentrum Paul Klee, Bern, Gift of Livia Klee

Art as Creation

left: Meister Bertram, Grabow Altarpiece, Creation of the Animals, (Detail with Elements of Paul Klee's *With Rainbows* and *Landscape With Golden Birds*), 1379–83, Hamburger Kunsthalle

No doubt you have heard about the Story of Creation.

That is the story in the Bible that tells how the world came to be. It says that Heaven and Earth were created first, and then bit by bit lots of other wonderful and necessary things were added: the sun, moon, and stars, the seas and oceans, the countless plants and animals, and, of course, mankind.

The Bible says that a great and unique Creator – God – thought it all up and created everything. How incredible! What an imagination! It is scarcely possible for us to grasp this idea using our reason!

The Bible says that everything this Creator came up with had never existed before. That means that God didn't copy something seen somewhere else. No, God **created** it all by drawing on something from within. Paul Klee did not believe everything in the Bible, but he was absolutely fascinated by the thought of Creation.

Field Rhythms, 1931,
private collection, Switzerland

As an artist, he did not consider himself to be God, but he thought of **art as creation** and of himself as the **creator of his art.**

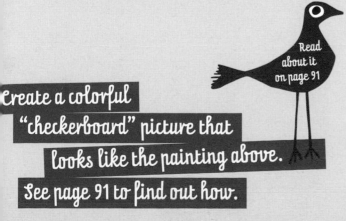

Read about it on page 91

Create a colorful "checkerboard" picture that looks like the painting above. See page 91 to find out how.

"Art is similar to Creation," said Paul Klee. He meant that just as God created the world and all life forms, **the artist also creates a world.** That artistic world is not one that already exists, but a completely new one. So Paul Klee never wanted to just copy or reproduce anything. Instead, he used every line and every spot of color to bring something new into being, to create something that was as unique as a creation of God.

Paul Klee felt that as an artist, one could easily use the unbelievable beauty of nature as a model. In order to judge the inventiveness of the being that had created nature, you did not have to meet God in person or even travel a long distance. All you had to do was open your eyes and look at the flowerbed in the garden, for example. Or look at ferns, fossils, crystals, birds, or insects.

You should observe objects carefully, not in order to copy them but in order to "see through" them. That means recognizing their nature and their boundless variety. By doing this, Klee felt, you could read nature as you could read a book: a book with lots of surprising elements. But the book of nature does not have a final page, because it is without limits and is inexhaustible.

The world is one vast rhythm of colors, shapes, movements, and different structures! Paul Klee wanted to show this in his paintings.

Read about it on page 91

"Is a work of art created in one go? No, it is built bit by bit, just like a house."
Have a go yourself, just as Paul Klee did when he made this picture.
Use circles, triangles, squares ... to build a colorful little world.

46

Red Bridge, 1928, Staatsgalerie Stuttgart

Painting in the Kitchen

What do painters do if they lack a space in which to paint? It's quite simple: they create a space anywhere they can find one. They may even use the kitchen! After Paul and Lily got married, they lived in a three-room apartment in Munich. It was just big enough: they slept in one room, lived in the second room, and placed Lily's grand piano – which she used to teach her pupils – in the third room. (Little Felix would live underneath the piano when he was older.) And where exactly was Paul's workplace, his studio?

It was where he actually felt most comfortable and spent most of his time: **in the kitchen.** After all, it was he who prepared food for the family every day (as Lily only knew how to cook one thing – a type of soup). Paul enjoyed cooking almost as much as he enjoyed painting, and sometimes his food looked as though it had been painted. No matter whether he created a painting or a new dish, he was the master of a new creation.

There were some advantages to painting his pictures next to the steaming pots and pans. For example, if he needed to stir the food, he just used his paintbrush!

Lucky Salad with Clover

Ingredients:
Clover leaves and
clover blossoms of
red and white clover
(season: June/July),
2 tablespoons oil,
2 teaspoons mint leaves
(finely chopped),
1/3 cup (75 grams) rice,
2 tablespoons orange juice
(freshly squeezed)

"White on Black" – Chocolate Pudding

Ingredients:
1 packet chocolate
pudding mixture,
1 pint (1/2 liter) milk,
2–3 heaped tablespoons
sugar

Read
about it
on page 91

Souvenirs à Bern – Swiss Cheese Tart

Ingredients for crust:
2 cups (250 grams) flour,
1/2 teaspoon salt,
1/2 cup (125 grams) butter
or margarine,
4 tablespoons water,
Margarine to grease the tin

Ingredients for filling:
2–4 cups (375–500 grams)
tomatoes,
1 large onion,
1 bunch chives,
6–8 thin slices white bread,
2 cups (200 grams) Emmental
cheese (sliced)

Ingredients for egg mixture:
3 eggs,
1 cup (250 grams)
whipping cream,
Pepper

To garnish:
Sesame seeds

Paul Becomes a "Blue Rider"

When a young father like Paul Klee lavishes all his attention on his son — cooking for him, making things for him, and generally taking care of him 24 hours a day — it sometimes happens that the father loses sight of what else is going on around him. That is what happened to Paul Klee. Although he lived in the "City of 5,000 Painters," he didn't see the other "4,999" artists for a long time! For example, it took many years before he noticed that one of the most famous Munich artists lived in a neighboring building: none other than **Wassily Kandinsky.**

People were constantly coming and going in and out of Kandinsky's apartment, and soon Paul Klee, too, was a regular guest. At first, he thought Kandinsky's paintings "very strange," because he had never seen anything like them.

On the one hand, Klee found the pictures strange. But on the other hand, he admired them for looking so childlike, crazily "primitive," and simple. Kandinsky's paintings looked like this not because the artist was **unable** to paint any other way, but because he did not **want** to paint any other way!

Kandinsky's paintings were completely new, not copied from anywhere else, and they did not appear to represent any real-life objects. Instead, the pictures showed what was not easily described: the inside, the nature, the **ESSENCE of things.** In other words, what they showed was different from what other paintings of the time showed!

Just as Kandinsky's pictures were jumbled, the painter's thoughts about art also jostled around in his head. For example, he was convinced that people could be changed if the art that surrounded them was changed. Paintings could sing and make the viewer's soul swing. How many other changes could then be possible!

And then Kandinsky, who loved blue, got together with other Munich artists, including Franz Marc, who loved to paint horses. This group called itself the "Blauer Reiter," which is German for **"Blue Rider."**

Together, the Blue Rider members plowed ahead with the aim of changing art: they wanted to hold art exhibitions and make a sort of yearbook of artwork. They wanted to open people's eyes (and hopefully also their souls) to modern art. They wanted to show pictures that had been created from their own innermost soul. Such pictures, they felt, were what art should be. Paul Klee felt the same way.

Franz Marc, *Blue Horse I (Detail)*, 1911, Städtische Galerie im Lenbachhaus, Munich

At the first exhibition of the "Blue Rider," Paul stood in front of a painting that he liked particularly. It showed a yellow cow that appeared to leap through the picture in a carefree manner. Surely nobody had ever painted an animal in this way before!

As Klee admired the work of the "Blue Rider," so too did Kandinsky admire Paul's pictures. Soon he invited Klee to become a member of the group. But Paul's art didn't seem to fit in with the colorful work of Franz Marc and Wassily Kandinsky. For Klee drew more than he painted; and he painted in black and white! Paul's new colleagues seemed far more advanced than he was when it came to using color in art.

Franz Marc, *Yellow Cow*, 1911, Solomon R. Guggenheim Museum, New York

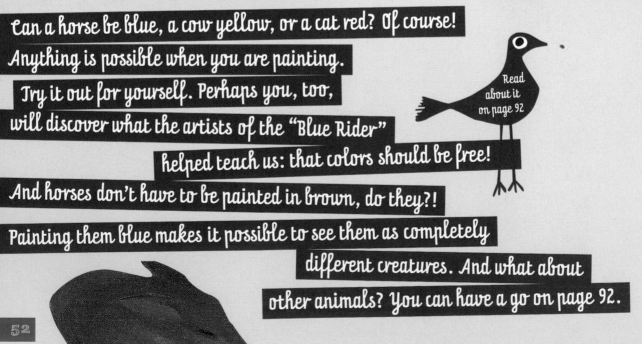

Can a horse be blue, a cow yellow, or a cat red? Of course! Anything is possible when you are painting. Try it out for yourself. Perhaps you, too, will discover what the artists of the "Blue Rider" helped teach us: that colors should be free! And horses don't have to be painted in brown, do they?! Painting them blue makes it possible to see them as completely different creatures. And what about other animals? You can have a go on page 92.

Read about it on page 92

Drawing
and Painting

Look here, a line …
And another one here …
and another …

―――――――――――――――

―――――――――――――――

―――――――――――――――

Three lines.

If lots of other lines were added to
these three, we wouldn't call them lines
anymore. We would say that they are a
"drawing." A drawing is nothing more than
a well-arranged collection of lines, and
often you don't need very many lines for
a little work of art.

Angelus Novus (New Angel), 1920,
The Israel Museum, Jerusalem

**Drawing is nothing more than
"taking lines for a walk,"** as Paul
Klee put it.

So drawing is about lines. Such lines are
usually black, and the background on
which they "go for a walk" is usually white.

What, then, do painters do? Obviously,
painters paint. But they usually take colors
for a walk, rather than lines, because
painting (unlike **drawing**) is mainly
about color.

The first pictures that Paul Klee painted looked something like this:

Quarry at Ostermundingen, 1908,
Städtische Galerie im Lenbachhaus, Munich

Fine, this picture may have been made with a paintbrush. But when paintings look like this, the painter is obviously missing something. And that something is:

C O L O R

Color? No problem. If a painter lacks colors, surely he or she could just run to the next paint store and buy the most vibrant red, the brightest yellow, and the coolest blue.

Read about it on page 92

Do you know all about colors?
Can you solve these colorful problems?
The answers are on page 92.

Yes, that would be one solution. But what's next? Once the painter is sitting at the drawing table with the paint tubes, he would realize: in order to paint, in order to create something that shows more than just colorful paint blotches placed next to one another, you need more than a paintbrush and paint. A painter who wants to use colors to show moods and arouse feelings in the viewer, or to show recognizable objects, must know all about color. The painter must be able **not only to see** colors, but to actually **feel** them deep inside!

And what if an artist notices that he doesn't have such feelings? What if colors leave him "cold" and he can't use them to show what he would like to show? What if, as Paul Klee said about himself, he finds it hard to **"get along with"** color? Well, that artist (and Klee WAS that artist) should pack his bags and get going to a place where he can learn to appreciate colors.

And where might that place be? Hard to say. In Bern? No! In France and Italy? Clearly not!
Where then?

Kairouan, *Before the Gate*, 1914,
Moderna Muset, Stockholm

August Macke, *Kairouan I*, 1914,
Bayerische Staatsgemäldesammlungen,
Munich

Trip to Tunis

Garden in the European Colony of St. Germain, 1914, The Metropolitan Museum of Art, New York

What about Africa?

Paul Klee had heard a lot about Tunisia. The light there, as Wassily Kandinsky had told him enthusiastically, is unlike the light anywhere else! And light has something to do with colors. So one day, Klee and his friends August Macke and Louis Moillet were having a conversation. When the conversation turned to Tunisia, it did not take them long to decide! Yes, they would travel to this country together.

Monday, April 6, 1914

"At midday, twelve o'clock, we went aboard … sailing through the harbor was like taking a stroll, very enjoyable … but that does not change the fact that the deck sometimes resembles a crooked roof on which every-thing slides around: men, women, and deck chairs … there are fewer and fewer passengers. But the three of us are cheerful …"

Tuesday, April 7, 1914

"Woke up with a view of the coast of Sardinia. The colors of the water and air are much more intense today than they were yesterday … Later, the first Arab city became clearly visible. Sidi-Bou-Said (…) The incarnation of a fairy tale … The first Arabs are not far away, on the shore. The sun has a dark power. The colorful clarity on land is promising …"

August Macke and Paul Klee with a guide in Kairouan, April 1914 (from a photo album of August Macke), 1914, LWL-Landesmuseum für Kunst und Kulturgeschichte, Münster

Wednesday, April 8, 1914

"My head is full of yesterday evening's impressions. Art-nature-me. Got to work straight away and painted using watercolors in the Arab quarter. (...) Then bought a couple of things in the souks. Macke praises the stimulus to spend money."

Thursday, April 9, 1914

"... Painted in the harbor. Coal dust in my eyes and in my watercolors ... To a concert arabe in the evening ... Pretty good belly dances. Doesn't exist at home ..."

Tuesday, April 14, 1914

"Spent the night at the house of a mean old Frenchwoman. Louis and Macke had a pillow fight in their shirts ... High oboe notes and tambourine beats lured us towards a snake charmer and a scorpion eater: a delightful street theater. The donkey was watching, too."

Easter Sunday, April 12, 1914

"The evening is indescribable. On top of everything else, the full moon came out. Louis tells me I should paint it. I say: it will be an exercise at best. Of course I must fail, faced with this nature..."

Easter Monday, April 13, 1914

"Painted and swam in the morning. A dung beetle saint does its work in front of me. I'll work like that, too, trying again and again ..."

With the Brown ▲, April 1915, Kunstmuseum Bern

Thursday, April 16, 1914

"Painted outside the city in the early morning, slightly diffused light, mild and clear at the same time. No mist, then painted inside. A silly guide created hilarity. August taught him German words, but the words that he taught him... Through the streets in the evening... Louis saw coloristic tidbits and I was supposed to record them because he says I can do it so accurately.

I'll stop working now. It penetrates so deeply and so gently into me, I feel it and become so confident, without effort.

Color has got me. I don't need to grasp at it. It has got me forever, I know it. This is the meaning of this happy moment: color and I are one. I am a painter."

"That doesn't really look like him yet!"

When Paul Klee painted a picture, working hard at creating a balanced composition by positioning one shape here and another shape there, something extraordinary could happen. The calm, friendly painter could become incredibly angry.

This happened when someone – not an artist – watched Klee painting a portrait. He then commented on the unfinished picture, saying:

"That doesn't really look like him yet!"

Paul would then take a deep breath, try to keep his cool, and say quietly to himself: **"Whether it does or it doesn't, I have to carry on building now ..."**

And he carried on "building" ... building his painting, his creation. After all, it was not Klee's aim to create an exact copy of his subject on the canvas!

What would be the point? This very man existed already! Why should he create someone else just like him? No, you don't need art to do that!

Paul was able to do much more than that with his art:

He did not want to create another image of something that was already visible. Instead, he wanted to make the invisible visible.

Black Knight, 1927, Kunstsammlung Nordrhein-Westfalen, Düsseldorf

Caspar David Friedrich,
View of the Elbe Valley (Detail), about 1807,
Staatliche Kunstsammlungen Dresden

"Art does not reproduce visible things, it makes things visible."

Does that make sense to you? Do you understand what Paul Klee is trying to say here?
Really?
Let's see ...

Let's use a tree as an example. A tree is a visible object. And the picture above shows what a tree looks like, right? It's a nice tree, everything about it is easily recognizable: its spreading treetop, its thick trunk ... The painter has reproduced everything that is visible with precision and has done so very well. No wonder that the painter's contemporaries admired him for it.

Making the Invisible Visible

But Paul Klee wanted something different. (Read the sentence at the beginning of this section once again.) In his pictures, he wanted to make something visible: he wanted to make the invisible visible!

Making the invisible visible was not a new idea in art. Other artists long before Paul Klee had made it their mission again and again to show things in their pictures that were not actually visible. One such artist depicted the wind, as you can see here:

The North Wind, Tacuinum Sanitatis,
14th century, Austrian National Library

Wait, stop! Is that supposed to be the wind? Isn't that just a fluttering scarf! Well spotted. The painter has chosen an easy way out, but what else could he have done? He could not do magic, after all!

But Paul Klee was different! When Klee painted a tree, he didn't just reproduce the tree as he saw it, making an image of it on his canvas using paint. Instead, he tried to show everything that is actually hidden from the eye, which cannot actually be seen. (A camera could record the visible in a photograph, anyway.)

Such as? Well, such as lots of things – for example, the flow of energy that runs through the whole tree and into its leaves. Paul also showed the power with which the tree's roots dig into the ground in order to withstand even the greatest of storms; the tree's ability to strive and grow upwards, towards the light, towards the sky; and the tree's usefulness as a home to birds and lots of other things ...

That is why trees in Paul Klee's paintings look completely different from earlier pictures of trees.

Now it is your turn:
Can you make something invisible visible?
Have a go, don't be afraid.
It's not important here
that it should actually look
like a visible object.

Plants, Earth and Air Empire, 1921, Albertina, Vienna

War!

Paul Klee as a Soldier, 1916,
Zentrum Paul Klee, Bern,
Gift of the Klee family

Warning of the Ships, 1917,
Staatsgalerie Stuttgart

In August of 1914, Paul wrote the alarming words in his diary: **"Outbreak of the world war."**

What had happened? Yes, it was true, war really had broken out. Lots of countries, including Germany, England, France, and Russia, had become involved in a tremendous fight with one another. One country wanted one thing, another country wanted another thing, and none of them was willing to withdraw its claims or to give in. And so a fight turned into a war and soldiers started to kill each other. Wasn't there a reason to be concerned? Not for Paul Klee. Like many others, he was absolutely convinced that Germany would emerge from the war as the winner after just a few days. He even felt that this war did not actually have anything to do with him, and it need not worry him.

But then, terrible things began to happen. First, Paul Klee's good friend August Macke, with whom he had spent an unforgettable time in Tunis, was killed. Macke was a soldier and was shot and killed at the age of just 27. And the killing did not end as quickly as had been expected at all. Two years later – the war was still going on – Klee also found out about the death of Franz Marc, his fellow painter, whom he admired so much. And on the same day (when it rains, it pours!) he received his own draft call: the order to go to war as a soldier himself.

How terrible! If only he had had Swiss citizenship – like his mother. But he did not, and so he had no choice: forward march! Paul did not lose his ability to laugh, though. He imagined that his uniform was a funny costume in which he now went to war, in which he would have to march for hours and hours.

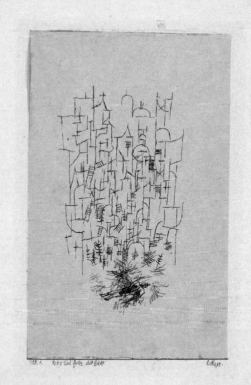

Death for the Idea, 1915,
Zentrum Paul Klee, Bern

But as it happened, things could have been a lot worse: the King of Bavaria himself had given the order that no more artists should be sent to the front. Too many of them had died already. So Paul Klee was allowed to paint airplanes and help the treasurer – and was even given the opportunity to paint his own pictures – instead of shooting at other men. And what does a painter paint when he is at war? Does he paint the war?

No, Klee did the very opposite. Nothing of this dreadful war would find its way into his art.

Interplay of Forces in a Lech River Landscape, 1917, private collection

1917. 56.

With the Rainbow, 1917,
private collection, Switzerland

Bauhaus Master

One morning in October 1920, the doorbell rang and the messenger gave Paul Klee a telegram. To his surprise, he read the following words:

"Dear Paul Klee. We unanimously invite you to join us as a master at the Bauhaus in Weimar."

These lines had been written by Walter Gropius, who had founded an art academy one year beforehand. The other "masters" who taught there had signed, too. Lots of them were famous artists, including the German-American painter Lyonel Feininger and the Swiss painter Johannes Itten.

Gropius's school, the "Bauhaus," was something completely new and spectacular: its makers wanted to redesign people's social lives, and in this way work on the "creation of the future." They wanted to reinvent houses and rooms, as well as the things you would find inside them: furniture, wallpaper, tableware, and even the pictures on the walls.

"Starting from zero" was their slogan, and lots of young people felt attracted to and stimulated by this idea, particularly because the First World War had been so destructive. They hoped that by changing the environment in which people lived, maybe they could change how those people conducted their lives. Of course, such change meant doing more than just hanging new pictures on the walls or drinking coffee out of new coffee cups.

Unstable Equilibrium, 1922, Zentrum Paul Klee

Gerrit Rietveld,
Red-Blue Chair, 1923

the Bauhaus, and his job was to lead one of the workshops. Most importantly, he was supposed to teach the Bauhaus students how to deal with color, lines, surfaces, and dots. All of these are important elements when it comes to creating a picture.

This work was completely new to him. Now he had to put into words the pictures and symbols that normally just bubbled out of him quite naturally!

It meant a completely new feeling for things that were created as visual objects: for everything that had form and color — for rooms, for furniture, for coffee cups, and for everything else.

"Starting from zero" meant something like: forgetting everything that had gone before! What should we do with old chairs, for example? Forget them! Start by thinking, looking inside yourself, and asking: is it not possible that people need completely different shapes for their chairs? Isn't it also possible that people need to transform other parts of their lives, such as their rooms and ultimately their thoughts and their souls? Paul Klee was now one of the masters at

Have you ever been so lost in thought that you have forgotten yourself? Perhaps you did not even notice it, or have already forgotten it. Ask your parents whether they have ever seen you looking completely lost in thought. Get ready to be surprised and astonished!

Like other Bauhaus teachers, Klee demanded of his students that they forget. He told them to leave behind everything that surrounded them in their memories. And most importantly, he told them to forget themselves! Yes, really! Bauhaus students were supposed to "reduce" their own selves – their own personalities – to nothing. They could then pretend to use their senses for the first time.

Klee's students were told not to think about wanting to make "art" when they sat in front of him. Paul was convinced that, if such thoughts were lurking about in their brains, nothing good would come out of it. Real art, he believed, could not be created from the desire for art alone.

How should it be done, then?
This is how Paul Klee did it with his students:
First, he threw a heap of old materials onto their worktables: old paper, cardboard, old wallpaper, steel shavings, glass …

1

2

3

4

Then each of the students was supposed to look at the material very carefully, touch it, smell it, take it apart, and compare the different bits. They needed to feel it without evaluating it, without saying "Oh, I like that!" or "Yuck! How unpleasant!" That's because such evaluations were not the point. The students were supposed to forget themselves, including their likes and dislikes. The students were supposed to **experience** the thing lying in front of them!
It was supposed to **stimulate their imagination!**
It was supposed to sharpen their senses!
It was supposed to astonish them!
And that leads to the question: **Why am I astonished?**

Yes, a heap of rubbish can provoke all of that … And anybody who had gone through and experienced all of these steps deep inside had the opportunity to become an artist and to create art.

Different materials are often combined with each other – not just in art, but also in everyday objects – for quite practical reasons. Yogurt pots made of plastic usually have an aluminum lid, and paper labels are stuck on glass bottles … Can you think of any other examples?

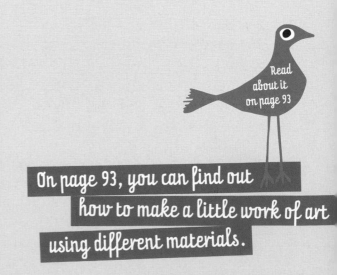

Read about it on page 93

On page 93, you can find out how to make a little work of art using different materials.

Paul Klee was a master of lines.

Using just one single line, he could create just about anything: a tree, an island, a boat ... See for yourself.

Doll by the Wayside, 1939, Zentrum Paul Klee, Bern

And Another Camel, 1939, private collection, Canada

Bell Angel, 1939, Zentrum Paul Klee, Bern

When Klee created these simple, primitive, childlike drawings, he was not particularly young himself. He was a grown man, more than 50 years old. But Paul didn't draw in this style because he COULDN'T draw any other way. He simply DIDN'T WANT to draw any other way!

His motto was:
It is possible to achieve a great deal with very little. Abundance is possible in simplicity, too!

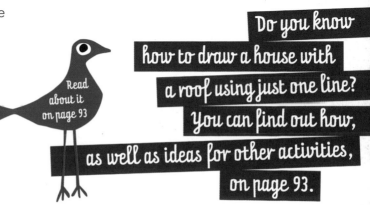

Read about it on page 93

Do you know how to draw a house with a roof using just one line? You can find out how, as well as ideas for other activities, on page 93.

"Journey to the Land of Better Understanding"

What happens when you send a dot 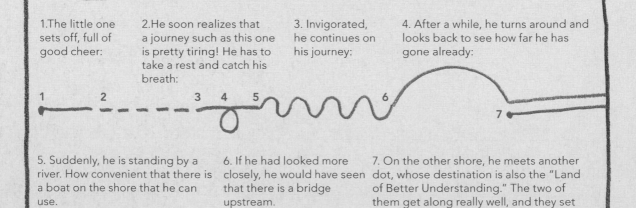 on a journey, ... on a journey to a very special place, the "Land of Better Understanding"?

1. The little one sets off, full of good cheer:

2. He soon realizes that a journey such as this one is pretty tiring! He has to take a rest and catch his breath:

3. Invigorated, he continues on his journey:

4. After a while, he turns around and looks back to see how far he has gone already:

5. Suddenly, he is standing by a river. How convenient that there is a boat on the shore that he can use.

6. If he had looked more closely, he would have seen that there is a bridge upstream.

7. On the other shore, he meets another dot, whose destination is also the "Land of Better Understanding." The two of them get along really well, and they set off together.

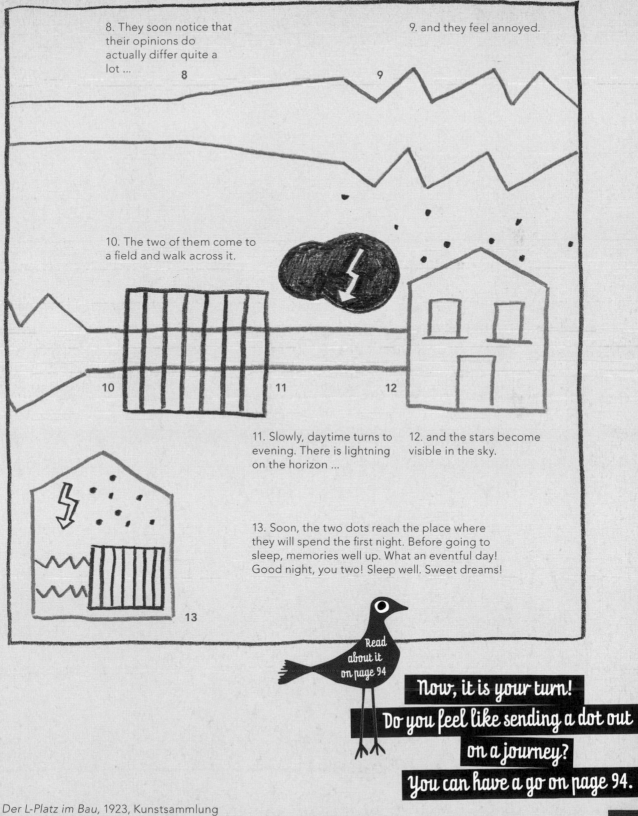

8. They soon notice that their opinions do actually differ quite a lot ...

9. and they feel annoyed.

10. The two of them come to a field and walk across it.

11. Slowly, daytime turns to evening. There is lightning on the horizon ...

12. and the stars become visible in the sky.

13. Soon, the two dots reach the place where they will spend the first night. Before going to sleep, memories well up. What an eventful day! Good night, you two! Sleep well. Sweet dreams!

Read about it on page 94

Now, it is your turn! Do you feel like sending a dot out on a journey? You can have a go on page 94.

Der L-Platz im Bau, 1923, Kunstsammlung Nordrhein-Westfalen, Düsseldorf

Do-It-Yourself Klee

Paul Klee liked to experiment using different materials and techniques. You can see the result of one of these experiments, which is made mainly of sand, here:

A picture made of sand like this one is more than just a nice souvenir of your last beach holiday. To find out which materials you will need to make a similar work of art, turn to page 94.

Cirrus, 1932,
Collection of Livia
Klee-Meyer, Bern

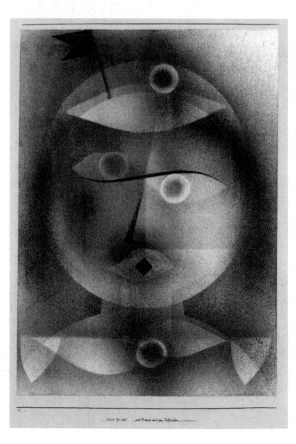

Pictures like this one were created during Klee's time as a teacher, first at the Bauhaus and then at the arts academy in the German city of Dusseldorf. Here, Paul Klee did not apply paint with a paintbrush or a pencil, but sprayed it on.

Try it out yourself. You can learn which materials you will need on page 94

The Mask with the Little Flag,
Bayerische Staatsgemäldesammlungen,
Munich

(from the Song of Solomon) second version, 1921,
Solomon R. Guggenheim Museum, New York

Spoken words can sound bright and
beautiful. Written words, too, can be made
to glow, as Paul Klee has done here.

Read
about it
on page 94

Have a go yourself.
You can find a couple
of pointers on page 94.

Bittersweet Island: There Are Two Sides to Everything

What would life be like on a desert island? On the one hand, it would be nice: no arguments with parents, brothers and sisters, or friends, and nobody would complain if you sang loudly or picked your nose. And of course there would not be any schools, either.

On the other hand, you would probably get lonely pretty soon without another human being around. And of course, you would be very busy just staying alive: as the only person there, you would have to collect rain water, catch fish, harvest coconuts, or do whatever a lonely inhabitant of a desert island has to do.

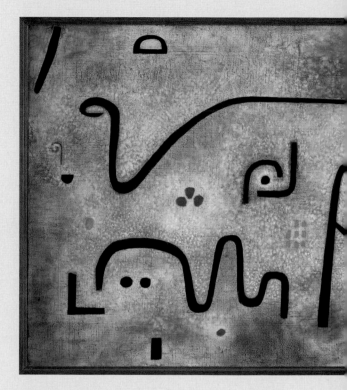

One thing is clear: such a life would be beautiful and tempting in some ways and, at the same time, frightening and dreadful in others. It would be both sweet and bitter at the same time.
Bittersweet.
And that is what Paul Klee named one of his pictures: Bittersweet Island, Insula Dulcamara.

Read about it on page 95

One can feel bittersweet, and one can also taste it. Can you imagine what bittersweet tastes like? You can find out more about it on page 95.

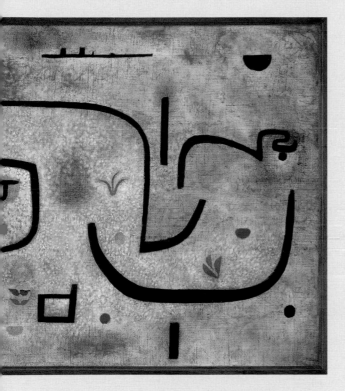

Insula Dulcamara (Bittersweet Island), 1938,
Zentrum Paul Klee, Bern

Yes, it is surprising, but it's true. Klee compared human life to an island because it often seemed to him that, just like an island in an ocean, all people are actually by themselves throughout their lives. That sounds sad, but it is understandable. For at the time that Paul was painting this picture, he was thinking a lot about his life and about death.

Strange things are happening on Paul Klee's bittersweet island: there are lots of mysterious symbols, a little bit like Arabic script or Egyptian hieroglyphics. And is that a friendly face looking out at us? And another one there? Yes indeed, some elements are familiar and likeable. But when it comes to reading the writing and solving the picture's riddle: no, nobody would be able to do that.

Paul Klee didn't want us to solve everything here. His image is actually about life. And what is life? Life is a sequence of experiences that are often mysterious and puzzling, some of which can perhaps never be fully unraveled.

Obviously, an island does not taste bittersweet. And you would never find an island called "Insula Dulcamara," no matter how long you sailed the seas in search of it.

So what does this picture mean? You already know this much about Paul Klee: he often recorded his deepest thoughts and feelings in his pictures. In the same way, Paul Klee is not actually describing an island in his picture. He is actually describing ... his life!

1939 AB8 . Engel im Kindergarten

Some Kind of Angel

It is a sad fact, but unfortunately one that cannot be changed: life is not endless, and every person has to die some day. Death is part of life, just as birth is. Lifetime on Earth is limited, and that is precisely why it is so incredibly precious.

When Paul Klee was 56 years old, he became sick with a terrible illness. The doctors did not know what to do and could not help him. All they could do was watch as he slowly dried up like a plant whose life force gradually ebbed away.

"Death is not a terrible thing, I have long since accepted it. Does anybody know what is more important: this life or the one that follows?"

Somebody who is facing death no longer sees only sunny days, blooming flowers, or cheerful birds. And because Paul Klee painted from deep inside his soul, it is understandable that his pictures changed toward the end of his life. He now made art that had titles such as "Outbreak of Fear," "Monster in Waiting," and "Dark Boat Journey."

And he drew lots and lots of angels. One was an angel called "Irgend," which means "Some Kind," whose presence he thought to be beautiful and comforting:

"Some day I shall lie in nothingness, beside Some Kind of Angel"

When you know that you haven't got much time left to do something, you can feel quite anxious. (Perhaps you have experienced something like this during an exam?)

You know that you should get to the point, finish what you are doing, and "draw a line" underneath it all. That is easier said than done. First, you would have to come up with everything that is essential and important. Then you would have to find solutions and put these down on paper skillfully. That is reason enough to chew nervously on your pencil.

Angel in the Kindergarten, 1939, Zentrum Paul Klee, Bern

But sometimes it is difficult to come to the end of something. Eating food or watching television, for example. And yet it is very important: finding the right moment to stop doing something, to come to the end, to draw a line underneath it.

That is what it was like for Paul Klee with his art. Towards the end of his life, his pictures were made up almost entirely of simple lines, as though he were practicing "drawing a line underneath" things.

Paul Klee's own life came to an end on June 29th, 1940. He died in Switzerland at the age of 60. He had returned to Switzerland after the National Socialists – the Nazis – had come to power in Germany and restricted the freedom of many German artists.

Words from Klee's diary are written on his grave, which is in the Schlosshalden-Friedhof cemetery in Bern:

"I cannot be grasped here and now. Because I live as much among the dead as among the unborn. Slightly closer to the heart of creation than usual. And still not nearly close enough."

Again Hoping, 1939,
Rosengart Collection, Luzern

1939MM15

Abfahrt des Abenteurers

*Departure of the Adventurers, 1939,
private collection, Germany*

Do You Know All About Klee?

2.

1.

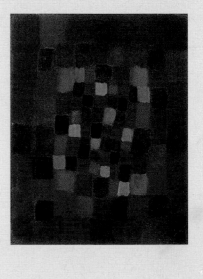

Read about it on page 95

Klee-Quiz

Sometimes, Paul Klee gave his pictures really crazy titles. But other times, Klee used titles that basically describe what can be seen in the pictures. Can you choose the correct three titles from this list of six and assign them to the paintings they belong to? You can check your answers on page 95.

"Three-Four Time Squared"

"Dreamtown"

"Green X Above Left"

"The Twittering Machine"

"Colourful Flowerbed"

"Family Walk"

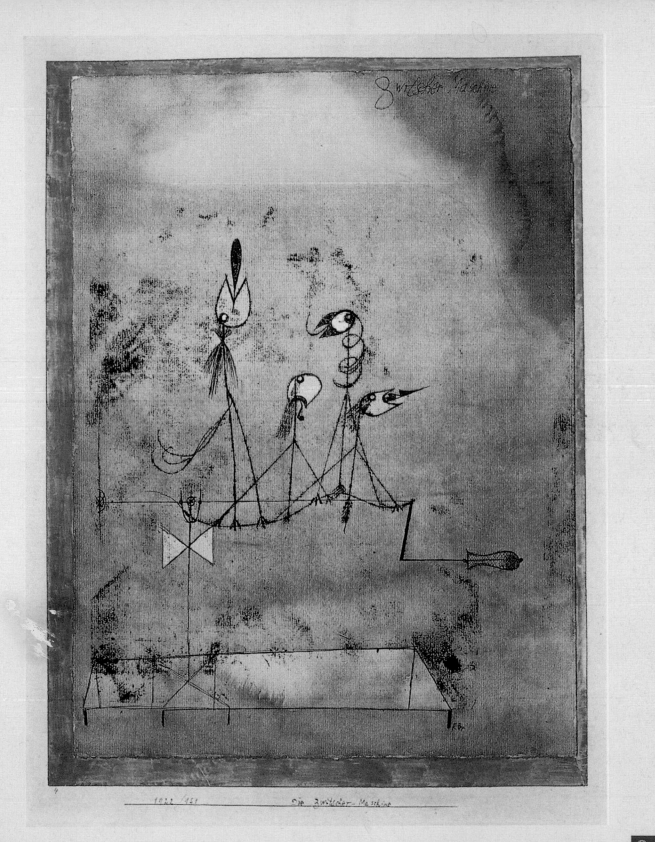

Klee-Quiz
Advanced Questions

Riddles and brain teasers
(After notes from Paul Klee's diaries and records)

Read about it on page 95

1. "What will you do when all you have left is life itself?"

2. "Why do you need a chair to understand a picture?"

3. What is the correct version of this proverb?
   Even a blind hen sometimes finds
   a) an egg
   b) a grain of corn
   c) a rooster

4. How do you think Paul Klee might have recreated this proverb as a joke?
   Even a blind hen sometimes finds
   a) an egg
   b) a grain of corn
   c) a rooster

5. What is this?

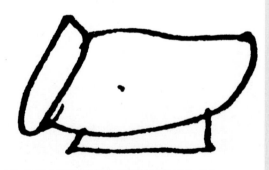

6. What did Paul Klee refer to as "bull's eyes" during his trip to Tunis?
   a) Fried eggs
   b) Olives
   c) Pomegranates

7.

Do you consider this square
a) … heavy
b) … light
c) … small
d) … big

Answers and Crafts Corner

Page 11

The special word

We are looking inside the following objects:
1. Clockwork (I), 2. Computer (M), 3. Red cabbage (A),
4. Earth (G), 5. Human body (E), 6. Onion (S)

So the special word is: IMAGES

A game with pictures

Try making pictures of things from your own unique
perspective. Just grab a camera and search for
unusual views of objects that you see every day.
You can do this inside your home or out of doors.
Your creations might look something like the photos
below. Can you tell what these images show?

1.   2.   3.

3. A piece of graffiti on a wall, showing a bear
2. A plastic sign stuck to a lamppost
1. A section of a traffic sign

You can even use such photographs to set up a game
with pictures at your next birthday party. To do this,
you'll need to take photos of objects in the area where
you will celebrate your birthday. (Don't go alone,
though: take a grownup with you.) Start right in front
of your front door, taking a picture of an object that
can be easily seen and clearly identified from the
doorstep. You might choose a door knob or a nearby
bush. For the second photograph, walk a short
distance from the front door and select the next
object. Follow a particular route in this way, taking
pictures as you go, and make a total of about 10 to 15
photographs. Choose the route so that it ends up in
a nice place, such as an ice cream parlor or a playg-
round.

Get the photographs printed at home and number
them in the correct order. To play the game, you can
split your friends into two teams and give each team
a set of the photographs. Tell the teams to find the
exact route you have "mapped out" with your pictures.
(Make the second team wait a while after the first
team has set off.) Those who successfully complete
the game can win an ice cream cone or some other
prize!

Page 13

The mysterious symbols

The bottom shape looks like a running man – but he's
missing arms, hair, and a nose! What do you think
the top two shapes resemble? Give your imagination
free rein.

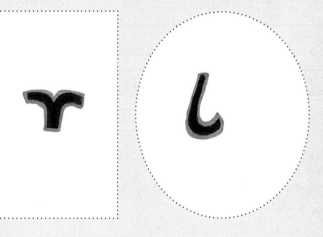

Make a herbarium (this word comes from the Latin "herba," which means plant)

You will need:
A plant, absorbent paper, a piece of black card, adhesive tape, tweezers, and a picture frame with glass

This is how it works:
First, you press the plant that will become part of your herbarium. It needs to end up not only flat, but also dry. This is particularly important when it comes to plants with colorful blossoms, because drying them allows their flower petals to stay colorful. For this reason, you must use very absorbent paper (blotting paper, watercolor paper, paper towels, etc.). Carefully position your plant on the absorbent paper, cover the plant with another piece of absorbent paper, and then place the whole thing between sheets of newspaper and a heavy book. Weigh down this heavy book with lots of other heavy books and leave the plant there for several days. Afterwards, you can remove the plant carefully, stick it onto the black card with adhesive tape, and frame it. You can even follow this procedure with many plants, sticking them all together in one frame. Don't forget to label and date each one.

1. c)
2. b) We say that people are "in clover" if they are very successful - especially if they have lots of money.
3. b)

You may know how to make **chocolate pudding** from a package. But you mustn't think that Paul Klee made pudding that way. He used a much more complicated method, and the dessert he created was simply delicious! You can make Paul Klee's chocolate pudding yourself.

You will need:
½ cup milk, 2 tablespoons cornstarch, 1 tablespoon cocoa powder, 1½ oz (50 g) dark chocolate, 1½ oz (50 g) sugar

This is how it is done:
Heat half of the milk together with the chocolate until the chocolate has melted and everything starts to boil (be careful: milk boils over very quickly!). Stir the rest of the ingredients into the other half of the milk, making sure that there are no lumps. Stir the cold milk mixture into the hot chocolate mixture and bring it all to boil again. Just don't forget to keep stirring! Then you can pour the pudding into little bowls, leave it to cool, and serve it.

Reverse-glass scratch painting

For your own reverse-glass scratch painting, you will need:
A small pane of glass (ask your parents if you can use an old picture frame), paintbrush, black ink, and a needle or other sharp object.

This is how it is done:
First, clean the pane of glass so that there is no greasy residue on it, such as fingerprints (window cleaner works well). Then paint a thin layer of black ink on one side of the glass and leave it to dry. Next, scratch a drawing into the black surface with the needle. Use the needle as though it were a pen. If you want to create a light area, scratch the ink away in several parallel lines. For a half-light area, scratch away fewer lines; and if you want an area to stay black, just leave the ink as it is. Once you have finished your drawing, place a sheet of white paper on top of it, turn the pane of glass over, and have a look at your artwork. Are you satisfied? You can use colored instead of white paper, or even multicolored paper. That will change the effect of your drawing dramatically! If the pane of glass is needed again by your parents, just wash off your artwork and return it to them.

A marble tabletop / a cloud-covered sky

Whether you are looking at a marble tabletop or a cloud-covered sky, there are always things to be discovered. Can you make out special images within the photographs shown here? Use a pencil and paper to draw what you see.

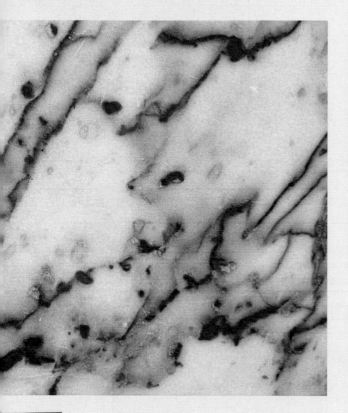

Answer: His two ears are missing!

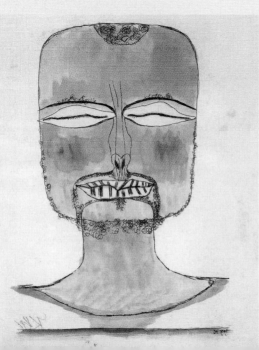

A simple musical instrument

Making a simple musical instrument yourself:
It could hardly be easier, and yet it's lots of fun. Start your own band with all the band members playing combs.

You will need:
A comb and a piece of transparent gift wrap (like the kind that is sometimes used to wrap flowers)

This is how it is done:
Cut a piece of the transparent gift wrap to roughly double the size of the comb. Fold it tightly over the comb, and hold the comb in your hands. Now hum a song, letting your lips vibrate while you hold the "wrapped" comb to your lips. This makes the gift wrap vibrate, and it creates a unique sound.

Lomolarm

C is the correct answer.

A short poem

This is how to write a simple poem made up of eleven words. It doesn't rhyme, but it can sound nice and interesting. Why not have a go yourself?

1. The first line should consist of one word. It might be a name, a color, a smell, or something like that.
2. For the second line, you will need two words that describe the word on the first line (they may explain what that first word does).
3. Three words go on the third line. They should describe the first word in another way (where does the word come from or what is it like?).
4. The fourth line is made up of four words. This is where you should write your personal thoughts about the word in the first line.
5. And the last line summarizes everything in one single word.

1. ....

2. ....

3. ....

4. ....

5. ....

A floor plan

In order to draw a "ground plan" of your room, try the following: First draw the walls, but make sure to leave a gap where the door is. Try to imagine what all the items of furniture in your room would look like if you were to view them from the top. For example, if you drew a bookshelf from the top, you wouldn't see the books it contains. You would only see the board that forms the top of the bookshelf. And what about your bed? Where is it? Draw it in its correct position in your room. You can make your drawing here.

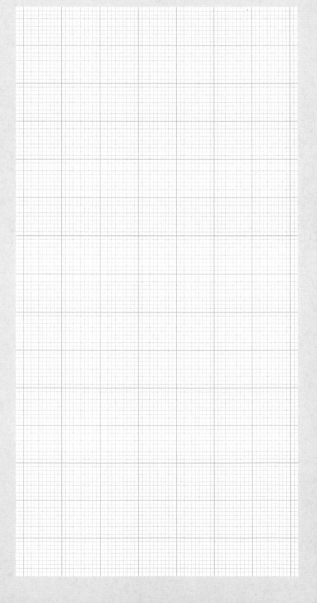

Three-dimensional drawings

You can make your own pictures three dimensional. Just assemble them as though they were little building blocks!

This is how it is done:
First, you need to collect little artworks such as drawings, postcards, old admission tickets, and so on. Ideally, they should be made of fairly stiff card (or you can stick them onto card if necessary).

Cut the pictures as shown in Illustration 1. Start your three-dimensional artwork with four pieces of card cut in this way: place two parallel to each other and then put a third and a fourth piece of card in the slits that are opposite one another. This gives you a foundation on which you can continue to build. Carry on building in this way to make a tower, a house, or any structure you like.

1

Locomotion

Would you like to make you pictures "move"? One way of doing this is to create a flip book. But you can also use another method called spinning locomotion.

You will need:
A wooden skewer, glue, and a photocopy of the four pictures on the left

This is how it is done:
Cut out the photocopies and fold each one exactly down the middle (vertically). Stick the photocopies to each other and around the skewer, as shown in the drawing. Hold the skewer in your hands and turn it backwards and forwards at high speed while you look at it. What can you see?

View from above

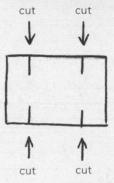

1   1

2   2

3   3

4   4

Page 36
Movements that we hardly notice

Many "movements" take place all the time that we hardly notice: thoughts that circle in our minds, clouds that drift in the sky, and text messages and e-mails that "fly" electronically through the air.

Page 38
Hidden objects

These are pictures of:
1. a towel, 2. rice, 3. paper, 4. milk,
5. wallpaper

Page 40
Observe nature

Observing nature and watching it grow

You will need:
A bean, a small amount of cotton wool, a saucer, and water

This is how it is done:
Place the bean in the cotton wool on the saucer and pour some water (not too much!) over it. Make sure that the cotton wool is always wet, and then wait to see what happens over the course of the next days. The result is something completely natural and completely wonderful: a plant will grow! But don't just observe this process, also describe it with words and little drawings. Then you will have something that always reminds you of that natural miracle.

Page 43
Hand puppets

Do you want to make your own hand puppets, just like Paul and Felix Klee? You can use the puppets to put on your own plays.

You will need:
Modeling clay that air-dries (you can find this in arts and crafts shops), a paint box, paintbrushes, pieces of fabric, pieces of wool, and a needle and thread

This is how it is done:
Use the clay to model something that looks like a head. You can use the puppets on page 43 as models (as you can see, they do not have to be perfect!). Make sure that you leave enough room for your index finger inside the "head," because that is how you are going to hold and move the head when the puppet is finished. Don't forget to make a neck, at the bottom of which there should be a little folded edge. This is where you will attach the cloak.

Once you are satisfied with the way the head looks, leave the clay to air-dry according to the package instructions. Once the specified amount of time has passed, you can paint and decorate the head using things like pieces of wool for hair, buttons for eyes, and so on.

To make the cloak, cut two shapes from old pieces of fabric. They should look something like this:

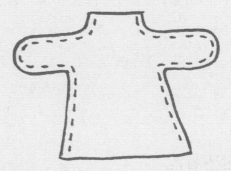

Don't forget that the size of the cloak should suit the head that you have made. Place one of the pieces of fabric onto the other and sew them together using simple stitches in the places marked on the drawing. Then slip the opening at the top (neck) over the neck of the puppet's head. Attach it using a piece of string. You can hide the string using a little piece of cloth for a "scarf."

If you need a simple puppet theater, place a broom handle over the backs of two chairs. Drape a blanket over the top so that you can hide behind it. And presto … your first actor has his very own stage. Have fun!

Hand puppet Paul

Paul portrayed himself in the puppet on the far left side of the second row.

Checkerboard picture

You can create a "checkerboard" picture yourself.

You will need:
A sheet of white paper (or, even better, stiff drawing board), pencil, paintbrush and box of watercolors, and a selection of other pens and pencils of various kinds.

This is how it is done:
Prepare the paper before you start to paint. You do this by drawing horizontal lines a few inches (or centimeters) apart, using a pencil. Next, draw vertical lines the same distance apart. This will create lots of squares on the paper. Then choose a square and color it any way you like. If you are sitting next to a friend, you might ask him or her to help you color! Try to end up with all of the squares looking different, no two the same. And don't rush: the two of you don't have to finish the whole thing in one visit. It takes time to create a great work of art!

Potato printing

Instructions for potato printing:
To make a picture like the one by Paul Klee, you'll need nothing but two potatoes, a potato-peeling knife, a box of watercolors, and paper.

This is how it is done:
Cut the potatoes in half. Use a pencil to mark the shape that you want your potato stamps to have. Then cut along the line using the knife, and remove a layer of the bit of the potato that is outside the shape. Now the potato piece should look something like this:

Your first stamp is ready. To make a picture like the one by Paul Klee on page 47, you will need more stamps with different shapes. Once you have made enough stamps, apply color to the surfaces of the stamps ... and off you go. Good luck! (Be careful when carving the potatoes, and ask for help if you need it.)

Painting in the kitchen

To make Lucky Salad with Clover:
Cook the rice and mix it with the oil and the orange juice while it is still hot. Wash the clover leaves carefully, removing the leaflets and mixing them with the rice and the mint.

To make Swiss Cheese Tart:
Mix the flour with the salt and the softened butter to form a smooth dough. Line a round pan (it's best to use a springform pan) with the dough, making a deep rim around the edge. Cover the dough with a layer of bread. Then add the cut tomatoes, chopped onion, chives, and cheese slices. Whisk the eggs with the cream, season the mixture with salt and pepper, and pour it over the top.

Sprinkle a few sesame seeds (if you have them) on the top and bake for about ½ an hour at 400 °F (200 °C) in a pre-heated oven. Serve hot or cold.

To make Chocolate Pudding:
See page 86.

Page 54

Colorful problems

Red + Yellow = Orange; Yellow + Blue = Green;
Brown – Red = Green

An artwork made of different materials

Picture frames are made of glass, cardboard, and either wood or metal. A light bulb also combines different materials. You can use materials in your own home or neighborhood to make a little work of art.

You will need:
The fork of a branch, pieces of wool, a darning needle, strong white yarn, different little objects (for example shells, buttons, or feathers), and such materials as aluminum foil, etc.

This is how it is done:
When you next go for a walk in the woods, choose a medium-sized forked branch: it will be in the shape of a big letter Y. Twist the strong white yarn around both arms of the branch, as shown in Illustration 1. Once you have done that, knot the ends of the yarn. Thread a piece of wool and weave this around the white yarn, as shown in Illustration 2. Attach little objects to the wool and weave them into your miniature artwork.

A house with a roof

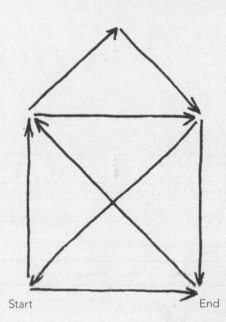

Start   End

Connect the dots

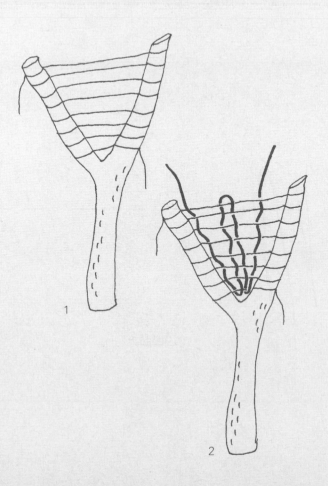

1

2

1. A business person (a dot) who is in a hurry goes quickly and directly from home (A) to work (B).

2. A person going for a stroll (a dot) wanders leisurely and unhurriedly from A to B. A dog (also a dot) goes along for the walk, bounding across the field.

1. To make a simple sand picture, which you can use instead of a postcard from your beach holiday, you will need:
A white card the size of a postcard, a strip of double-sided adhesive tape the length of the card, and some sand, pens, and coloring pencils

This is how it is done:
Place the card horizontally and color it in. For example, you can use colors that look like a sunset by the sea. Leave a strip a couple of inches (or centimeters) wide at the bottom of the card. Wait for the colors on the card to dry. Next, stick the adhesive tape along the length of the bottom edge, remove the plastic film that covers it, and dip your card into some dry sand. The sand will stick to the tape and, together with your coloring, look like a beach at sunset!

2. Make a spray painting with:
An old toothbrush, a small sieve, a box of watercolors, a little water, scissors, and several pieces of paper

This is how it is done:
First, cut simple stencil shapes (a heart, for example) from the pieces of paper. Place the paper heart on a complete sheet of paper. Coat the toothbrush with some water and then with watercolor. Brush the toothbrush along the sieve (away from your body) over the paper heart, so that a fine spray of paint is formed. Then leave the paint to dry. The paper will still be white in the place where the heart was. For the next round of spray painting, move the heart a little bit to one side and do it all over again. Try out different shapes and different colors. Perhaps you want to have a go at a design like the one on page 74?

3. Create a word picture with:
A piece of squared paper, black pencil, and coloring pencils or pens

This is how it is done:
On a sheet of squared paper (or paper with squares already printed on it), mark out a square in which you are going to write. Write whatever you like into this square in large, even letters. Make sure that the letters go all the way to the edges and bump into each other, like in Paul Klee's picture on page 75. Write in capital letters only. You don't need to bother with punctuation or spaces between individual words. Once you have finished, color the spaces between the letters in different colors until the entire background is colored in. Don't you think this would make a good greeting card?

Bittersweet taste

Have you ever eaten a grapefruit? If you taste one, you will know what "bittersweet" tastes like. They are difficult to peel, so the easiest way to eat them is this: place the fruit so that the stalk is either at the top or at the bottom, and cut it in half horizontally. Put each half in a bowl and sprinkle a little sugar on top. You can scoop out the grapefruit segments with a spoon. **Enjoy!**

Page 82/83
Klee-Quiz

1. *Green X Above Left*, 1915,
   private collection, Switzerland
2. *Family Walk*, 1930,
   Zentrum Paul Klee, Bern
3. *Colourful Flowerbed*, 1923, Kunsthaus Zürich
4. *The Twittering Machine*, 1922,
   Museum of Modern Art, New York

Klee-Quiz advanced questions

The (not always entirely serious) answers are:

1. Work as a (nude) model for life-drawing classes.

2. Because you need something to sit on, so that your tired legs don't distract your mind while you are thinking.

3. The correct answer is b), and that makes sense because a chicken looks for something that it can eat.

4. Paul Klee uses this saying in a way that makes no sense at all: Even a blind chicken sometimes finds an egg! As if chickens would go looking for eggs!

5. Felix's chamber pot, drawn by Paul Klee.

6. The correct answer is a).

7. In answer to the question of whether the illustrated square is heavy or light – small or big – let's hear what Paul Klee had to say:

"If I ask, 'Do I consider this square to be heavy or light', there is not just one answer. This is because, if I answered 'light!' and then added another, much smaller square to it, my premature answer would immediately become incorrect. So, we can say that the big one is heavy in comparison to the small one, and the small one is light in comparison to the big one. Relativities."

Silke Vry, graphic designer, archaeologist, and art historian, is the successful author of many children's books. She lives with her family in Hamburg. She has published several books with Prestel, including "Trick of the Eye."

Library of Congress Control Number is available; British Library Cataloguing-in-Publication Data: a catalogue record for this book is available from the British Library; Deutsche Nationalbibliothek holds a record of this publication in the Deutsche Nationalbibliografie; detailed bibliographical data can be found under: http://dnb.d-nb.de

Front cover:
Paul Klee, *The Bavarian Don Giovanni*, 1919, The Salomon R. Guggenheim Museum, New York, photo: akg-images

Picture credits:
p. 5, p. 9, p. 18, p. 21 top, p. 38, p. 39 left, p. 48–49, p. 70, p. 85 left, p. 87 top left, p. 87 top right, p. 93 left: Silke Vry; p. 6 top, p. 7: M. Vollenweider & Sohn, Bern, Zentrum Paul Klee, Bern, Schenkung Familie Klee; p. 6 bottom: Emil Nicola-Carlen, Bern, Zentrum Paul Klee, Bern, Schenkung Familie Klee; p. 12, p. 76–77: Artothek; p. 14 right: Zentrum Paul Klee, Bern, Schenkung Familie Klee; p. 16 bottom, p. 20–21: private collection Switzerland, Depositum im Zentrum Paul Klee, Bern; p. 17, p. 22, p. 28 left, p. 28–29, p. 32, S. 68, p. 71 left, p. 71 right, p. 78, p. 82 top right: Zentrum Paul Klee, Bern; p. 19, p. 37, p. 40, p. 43, p. 84: Zentrum Paul Klee, Bern, Schenkung Livia Klee; p. 20 top, p. 39 right, p. 64 left: Zentrum Paul Klee, Bern, Schenkung Familie Klee © Klee-Nachlassverwaltung, Bern; p.33: akg-images

Prestel, a member of Verlagsgruppe Random House GmbH

Prestel Verlag, Munich
www.prestel.de

Prestel Publishing Ltd.
4 Bloomsbury Place
London WC1A 2QA

Prestel Publishing
900 Broadway, Suite 603
New York, NY 10003

Paul Klee, *Church, the Clock with Invented Numerals*, 1883/84, Zentrum Paul Klee, Bern

www.prestel.com

Translation Jane Michael
Editor Brad Finger
Picture editor Katharina Knüppel
Design Katarzyna Roy
Coverdesign SOFAROBOTNIK
Production Ulrike Wilke
Art direction Cilly Klotz
Printing and Binding Neografia, Martin
Printed in Slovakia

Verlagsgruppe Random House
The FSC®-certified paper Hello Fat Matt 1,1 has been supplied by Condat, Le Lardin Saint-Lazare, France.

ISBN 978-3-7913-7077-4